SNOT, POOP, VOMIT, AND MORE:

THE YUCKY BODY BOOK

Alvin and Virginia Silverstein
and
Laura Silverstein Nunn

Illustrated by Gerald Kelley

Library of Congress Cataloging-in-Publication Data:

Silverstein, Alvin.

    Snot, poop, vomit, and more : the yucky body book / by Alvin Silverstein, Virginia Silverstein, and Laura
Silverstein Nunn.

        p. cm. — (Yucky science)

    Summary: "Explores 'yucky' things about the human body, including earwax, gas, bodily wastes, and
more"—Provided by publisher.

    Includes bibliographical references and index.

    ISBN 978-0-7660-3318-4

    1. Human physiology—Juvenile literature. I. Silverstein, Virginia B. II. Nunn, Laura Silverstein. III. Title.

    QP37.S545 2010

    612—dc22

                        2009012280

Printed in the United States of America

052010 Lake Book Manufacturing, Inc., Melrose Park, IL

10 9 8 7 6 5 4 3 2 1

To Our Readers: We have done our best to make sure all Internet Addresses in this book were active and
appropriate when we went to press. However, the author and the publisher have no control over and assume no
liability for the material available on those Internet sites or on other Web sites they may link to. Any comments or
suggestions can be sent by e-mail to comments@enslow.com or to the address on the back cover.

♻ Enslow Publishers, Inc., is committed to printing our books on recycled paper. The paper in every book contains
10% to 30% post-consumer waste (PCW). The cover board on the outside of each book contains 100% PCW. Our
goal is to do our part to help young people and the environment too!

Illustration Credits: © 2009 Gerald Kelley, www.geraldkelley.com

Photo Credits: Dennis Kunkel Microscopy, Inc./Visuals Unlimited, Inc., p. 24; Dr. Wolf Fahrenbach/Visuals
Unlimited, Inc., p. 14; Scimat/Photo Researchers, Inc., p. 34; Susumu Nishinaga/Photo Researchers, Inc., p. 26;
Tim Vernon, LTH NHS Trust/Photo Researchers, Inc., p. 38.

Cover Illustration: © 2009 Gerald Kelley, www.geraldkelley.com

Enslow Publishers, Inc.
40 Industrial Road
Box 398
Berkeley Heights, NJ 07922
USA

http://www.enslow.com

CONTENTS

What's Yucky?   *page 5*

CHAPTER ONE
Got Gas?   *page 7*

CHAPTER TWO
What's That Smell?   *page 12*

CHAPTER THREE
Skin Stuff   *page 18*

CHAPTER FOUR
Puking   *page 25*

CHAPTER FIVE
When You Gotta Go   *page 31*

CHAPTER SIX
Eew! Goo!   *page 36*

CHAPTER SEVEN
What's That Gunk?   *page 41*

Words to Know   *page 45*
Further Reading   *page 47*
Internet Addresses   *page 47*
Index   *page 48*

What's Yucky?

Did you know that every time you cough or sneeze, spit goes flying out of your mouth? Or when you wipe a runny nose on your sleeve, you're actually leaving a trail of snot? Eew! And what's that gooey stuff in your eyes after you wake up in the morning? Eye boogers? Gross!

Your body does yucky things like these every single day. Have you ever taken a look at your poop after you go to the bathroom? It not only looks gross, but it really stinks! Even after you leave the bathroom, the stinky poop smell lingers. You didn't always think poop was yucky. This is something you learned as you got older. A toddler with a dirty diaper may scoop up handfuls of poop and happily fingerpaint walls and furniture. Older kids and adults take one sniff and say, "Eew!"

People in different parts of the world may have different ideas about what's yucky, too. For example, most Americans find body odors unpleasant. They spend more than 2 billion dollars each year on perfumes and underarm deodorants to make themselves smell better. But many people in other countries find natural body odors attractive.

In this book, we'll discuss lots of yucky things about your body—the ways it can smell, the funny noises it makes, and all things gooey.

Got Gas?

EXCUSE ME!

Do you ever get in trouble for burping at the
dinner table? Your parents might say it's bad
manners. And yet, burping is normal. Everybody
does it—but not because it's a funny noise. It's
something that your body *has* to do. When you
burp, your body releases a buildup of gas. If you
try to keep yourself from burping, that built-
up gas can't escape—and you may feel awful.
Burping can actually make you feel better.

Why do you burp so much after drinking
soda? That's because soft drinks contain a gas
called carbon dioxide. It's what makes soda so
fizzy. If you shake up a can of soda and then open
it, bubbly soda sprays out of the top and spills

over the sides. Inside the can, the carbon dioxide was under pressure, which squeezed the gas into a small space. Opening the can released the pressure and the gas exploded out.

The same thing happens in your stomach when you drink soda. A round muscle at the top of the stomach opens to let in a mouthful of soda and then closes tightly. Your stomach stirs up the soda. The carbon dioxide pressure builds up. Then the muscle opens and the gas explodes out of your stomach. Up it goes, into your mouth, and then escapes with a sudden loud noise.

You don't need a soft drink to make you burp. People tend to swallow air when they eat or drink.

Yikes! The Guinness World Record for the loudest burp is 104.9 decibels (dB), set in 2004 by a man in London. Compare that to the noise of a vacuum cleaner (80 dB), a chain saw (100 dB), a rock concert (120 dB), and a jet engine (130 dB)!

104.9dB

100dB

The air builds up pressure in the stomach until the muscle at the top pops open.

WHO FARTED?

Even if you don't hear it, you can often tell when someone around you has farted. The smell is unmistakable. Just like a burp, farts can be embarrassing. But they are a natural part of life and help to keep you healthy.

Burps and farts are both caused by gas under pressure. But what makes you fart has more to do

with your intestines than your stomach. Instead of
"exploding" out of your mouth as a burp does, gas
bubbles travel through the intestines, where food
is digested (broken down). Eventually, the gas is
pushed out your butt.

Most farts aren't smelly. But if a fart does
stink, it's probably because of something you ate.
Stinky farts are usually caused by eating foods
such as beans, broccoli, and cabbage. These foods
are "gassy" because they cannot be completely
digested by your body. Microscopic bacteria that

Would You Believe. . . ?

The average person farts about fourteen times a day. Eating a lot of "gassy" foods can make people fart even more. Some health conditions and medicines can also make people produce extra gas.

live in your intestines break down these food materials. The gas they produce smells like rotten eggs because it contains stinky sulfur compounds.

Some farts just leak out, without making any noise. (They may still be very smelly, though.) How loud a fart is depends on how fast the gas is moving and how tightly the muscle in your butt is closed.

Have you ever tried to keep from farting? It's not easy. Sometimes you can't stop it. But if you *can* keep it from escaping, the gas might build up until you feel gas pains in your belly. Like burping, farting releases that pressure. So afterward, you feel better.

CHAPTER TWO

What's That Smell?

P.U.! STINKY FEET!

Do people say "P.U.!" when you take off your shoes? What makes feet smell has a lot to do with how sweaty they get. On each foot, you have more than 250,000 tiny organs called sweat glands. These glands pour out a watery mixture from openings in your skin called pores. In just one day, each foot can pour out more than two cups of sweat! But sweat itself does not have a stinky odor. It is mostly water and salt. The real culprit is the bacteria that feed on the sweat. Bacteria leave behind waste products that give off a "cheesy" smell.

You have sweat glands all over your body. The palms of your hands have about the same number of sweat glands as your feet. So why do your feet get smelly but your hands don't? That's because the sweat on your hands can evaporate into the air, but the sweat inside your socks and shoes is trapped. Bacteria like to grow in dark, damp places, especially inside sweaty sneakers. There they feast on dead skin cells and oils, and they multiply. At the end of a busy day, you take your shoes off and—yuck! Bacteria have been busy all day, too, making your feet stink!

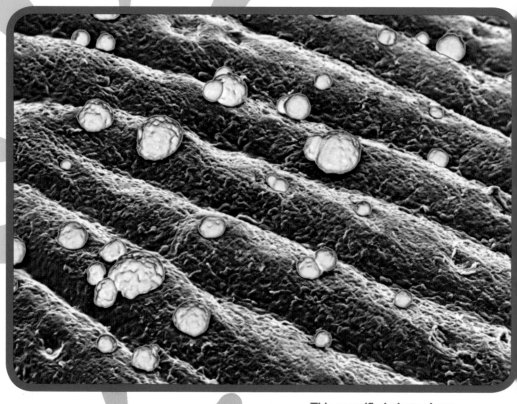

This magnified photo shows sweat coming from the pores on a human fingertip. You have pores like these all over your body!

Yikes! Researchers have found that some foot odor is produced by the same bacteria that are used in making cheeses.

OH, NO! B.O.!

When you run around in gym class, you can get really sweaty. Just one whiff from your armpits might make you shout, "Stin-ky!" But the body odor you have after gym class is caused by *different* sweat glands than those that cause stinky feet.

You have two kinds of sweat glands. The glands that lead to stinky feet are found on the palms of the hands, soles of the feet, and the forehead. The other sweat glands are found mostly on hairy parts of the body, such as the armpits.

Yikes! In the Middle Ages, girls gave their sweethearts "love apples." These were peeled apples that they had kept in their armpits to soak up underarm sweat.

These glands don't become active until the teen years. That's when special chemicals called hormones are released. The hormones make these glands produce thick, sticky sweat with lots of chemicals.

Body odor is produced by bacteria on the skin that feed on chemicals in the sweat. Underarm hair holds moisture, helping bacteria to grow. So sweat in the armpits is especially smelly.

DRAGON BREATH

Bad breath is at its worst when you wake up in the morning. You may have had minty fresh breath the night before, after brushing your teeth. But now you have "morning breath." What happened while you were sleeping? Once again, you can blame it on bacteria—this time in your mouth.

Bacteria live in your mouth all the time. During the day, your mouth is constantly making saliva (spit). Saliva washes the bacteria away from your teeth and gums. But while you sleep, the flow of saliva slows

Do You Have Bad Breath?

Unless someone tells you, it's hard to know when you have bad breath. That's because you quickly get used to any smell that you are around constantly. So you don't even notice it.

down *a lot*. Then the bacteria feed on leftover food particles and skin cells from the lining of your mouth. They leave behind waste products that contain smelly sulfur chemicals. So you wake up with stinky breath.

Bad breath can happen any time of the day, not just in the morning. It can be caused by not enough brushing and flossing, which leaves food particles in the teeth. Certain foods, such as onions and garlic, can give you bad breath. These foods contain very smelly oils. After eating these foods, the oils may stay in your saliva. They are also carried to your lungs, and then out through your mouth when you breathe. Spicy foods can cause bad breath, too. Smoking can also make a person's breath smell bad.

CHAPTER THREE

Skin Stuff

WHO'S GOT ZITS?

Many teenagers get zits. That's because of the flood of hormones in their bodies. The hormones act on tiny organs in the skin called oil glands. These glands ooze out an oily substance that keeps your skin and hair soft and smooth.

A teenager's hormones make the oil glands overactive. The extra oil clogs up the pores, especially on the face, neck, and back. Then skin bacteria that feed on the oil multiply and cause trouble. Trapped inside the pore, oil, bacteria, and dead skin cells build up and form a little swelling. This is the start of a zit, or pimple. A breakout of pimples, especially on the face, is called acne.

A bulging, clogged-up oil pore that stays closed will have a white center. It is called a whitehead. If the clogged pore is open, the top can darken into a blackhead. Sometimes the pore breaks open under the surface. Then oil, bacteria, and dead skin cells leak into the skin. The body's defenses react to this invasion, resulting in redness, swelling, and pus—a pimple develops.

It's a Myth!

Pimples are not caused by eating foods such as chocolate or greasy French fries. A dirty face doesn't cause zits either, since they form inside the skin.

BUMPS AND LUMPS

Did you know you can get warts from someone who has them? Warts are caused by viruses, tiny germs much smaller than bacteria. (Colds and the flu are caused by viruses, too.) Wart viruses may sneak inside your skin through a tiny cut or scratch on your hands or feet. Then they make skin cells multiply like crazy, piling up in extra layers. Eventually, a cauliflower-looking wart develops. Warts most often grow on the hands, feet, and face.

Most warts won't make you sick. But they can be yucky looking, so many people can't wait to get rid of them. After a while, warts usually go away on their own. But there are medicines that can remove them faster.

Warts are usually light-colored. But your skin may also have some darker-colored lumps and bumps. These are called moles. Like warts, they are formed by skin cells that keep multiplying until they pile up. But moles aren't caused by a virus. They usually appear on skin that has been in the sun.

It's a Myth!

You can't get warts from touching a toad. Toads have wartlike bumps on their skin, but they are not caused by the virus that causes warts in people.

Would You Believe...?

In eighteenth-century Europe, moles were considered a sign of beauty. Women who didn't have moles pasted "beauty marks"—artificial moles—on their faces. Today, some popular movie stars and fashion models are known for their facial moles. But some people think moles are ugly. Pictures in children's books often show a "wicked witch" with a large, hairy mole on her nose.

Some moles are flat. Others are raised lumps, like warts. Sometimes moles have hairs growing out of them.

IT'S SNOWING!

Dandruff is basically dead skin cells. This is normal. Your skin flakes off dead cells all the time. Usually you don't notice them because they're so tiny. But teenagers may get "flaky" more often than other people. That's because, thanks to their hormones, glands in the scalp make too much oil. The extra oil traps dead skin cells, and they clump together into bigger, more noticeable flakes.

A fungus might be to blame for dandruff. The fungus feeds on the oils on the scalp. Normally, it takes about a month for new skin cells to form. But on a scalp invaded by this fungus, new skin cells form much faster—in as little as eleven days!

This makes dead skin cells flake off much faster, too. Chemicals from the fungus may also make your scalp itchy.

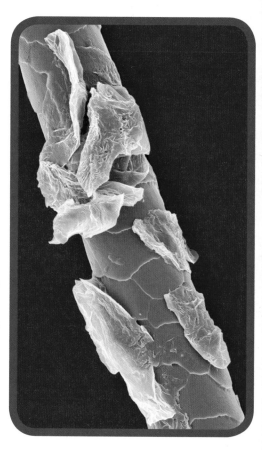

This photo, taken through a microscope, shows dandruff on human hair. The purple part is the dandruff. (The colors were added to the photo to show the difference more clearly.)

Would You Believe...?

When you shake someone's hand or wash your hands, you may lose as many as 40,000 dead skin cells in one minute! Your body makes new skin cells all the time to replace the dead ones.

CHAPTER FOUR

Puking

FEELING DIZZY

If you get sick to your stomach when you zoom through the twists and turns of a roller coaster, you know what it's like to have motion sickness. You probably get the same feeling when you spin around in a circle really fast, ride a merry-go-round, or ride in a car, airplane, or boat.

The reason you may get dizzy or nauseous (feel like you have to throw up) in these situations is that your brain is getting confusing messages.

Your body has different ways of telling whether you are right-side-up or upside down, turning, or standing still. Of course your eyes can tell you a lot. But your ears give you important information as well.

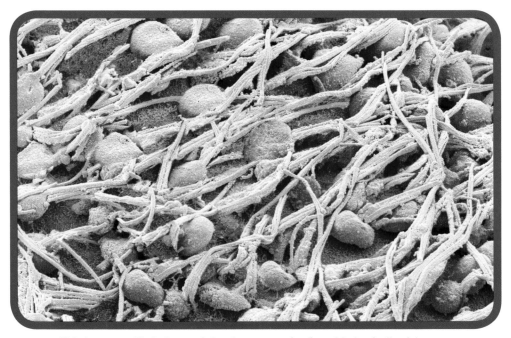

This is a magnified photo of the tiny stones (red) and hairs (yellow) in your ears that tell your brain about your body's position. (This photo was colored to show the difference more clearly.)

Two little "bags" deep inside each ear are lined with tiny hairs. These bags are filled with fluid and some tiny stones. The stones settle to the bottoms of the bags and touch the tiny hairs. If you bend over or turn, the ear stones will tumble until they rest on a different set of hairs. These hairs send messages about your position to your brain.

Each ear also has three curved tubes filled with fluid. When you bend or turn, the fluid in these tubes sloshes around, which sends a message to your brain that you have changed your position.

Your brain receives messages from nerves in your joints, too. That is how you know when your arms and legs move, even if your eyes are closed.

People may get motion sickness when the messages from the different senses don't agree. For example, if you are reading in a moving car, your eyes say that you are not moving but your ears say that you are. The result: you feel dizzy, your head hurts, your stomach feels queasy, and you may even throw up.

Would You Believe...?

The jerky movements in video games can make some people dizzy or nauseous.

THROWING UP

Normally, the food you eat takes a one-way trip down your throat, into your stomach, and on through the intestines, where it is digested. But if you have germs in your stomach or intestines or eat spoiled food, your body tries to get rid of the "bad stuff." The muscles in the stomach and intestines start to tighten, so much that it hurts!

Yikes! Your stomach acid is so powerful that it could burn a hole in a carpet or eat away the iron in a nail. So why doesn't it damage your stomach? Because the cells in the stomach lining are protected by a coating of thick, gooey mucus (slime). Your throat does not have this protective coating.

Instead of sending the food along the digestive tract, the muscles push the partly digested food back up. Then the muscle at the top of the stomach pops open, and you throw up (vomit or puke). Whatever you swallowed earlier comes gushing out of your mouth.

After you throw up, your throat probably hurts. That's because some of your stomach acid came up along with

the food you ate. The stomach acid burns your throat on the way up.

Throwing up is sometimes a good thing. It is your body's way of getting rid of poisons, germs, and other possibly harmful substances.

The color, taste, and smell of puke (the stuff you throw up) may vary, depending on what you ate. If you throw up blueberry pie, for example, your puke will be blue. Usually, puke smells pretty bad. That's because it contains partly digested foods that your body has started to break down.

When You Gotta Go

GOTTA PEE!

You're in a rush. If you don't leave right away, you'll miss the school bus. But—oh, no! You've got to pee! At times like that, peeing seems like just a bother. Actually, though, peeing is saving your life.

If you drink a lot of water, you will probably have to go to the bathroom a short time later. Pee (officially called urine) is about 95 percent water. But getting rid of water is only part of what peeing is all about. It's your body's way of flushing out poisons.

Urine is produced by your kidneys. These organs are like a pair of nonstop washing machines. They filter and clean your blood, keeping it free from waste products that might harm the body. The main waste product is a chemical called ammonia. This chemical is also found in some household cleaning products!

If all that ammonia were dumped into your bloodstream at once, you would be poisoned. Instead, your body changes ammonia to a less harmful chemical called urea. Urea makes up nearly 5 percent of your pee.

When you were a baby, you had to wear diapers. As you got older, you learned to control the muscles that hold in the pee until you get to the bathroom. Your body stores it in a baglike

Why Does Pee Stink?

Fresh pee has very little smell. But one whiff of a dirty public restroom can make you want to hold it in until you get home! Why does old pee stink? Blame it on bacteria. They break down urea, forming ammonia. That's what gives off the strong "urine smell."

organ called the bladder. You may sometimes have an accident and pee in your pants if you are very busy and let your bladder get too full.

GOTTA POOP

Have you ever taken a good look at your poop? It looks pretty solid, doesn't it? Actually, it's about 75 percent water!

Poop (also known as feces) is formed in your intestines, from the leftovers of the last few meals you ate. Food is digested in the small intestine.

As the undigested stuff moves on through the large intestine, your poop loses water. The more time poop spends there, the drier it becomes.

People with diarrhea have very loose, watery poop, and they have to go to the bathroom a lot. That's because the poop didn't spend enough time in the large intestine. On the other hand, constipation happens when food wastes stay in the large intestine too long, losing more and more water. The poop becomes dry and hard, and it is painful to push out of the body.

This is what poop looks like under a microscope! The brightly colored parts are different types of bacteria. (This photo was colored to show the different types of bacteria.)

Why Does Poop Stink?

Poop often stinks because the bacteria feeding on it produce various gases, including sulfur compounds, which create a rotten-egg smell.

What's in poop, besides water? About one-third of it is dead bacteria—the ones that didn't survive while trying to break down the food in your small intestine. The stuff you can't digest, such as plant fiber, makes up another third of poop. Fiber helps keep the poop moving along on the way out of your body. The last third is a mixture of fats, dead cells, salts, and live bacteria.

CHAPTER SIX

Eew! Goo!

GLOBS OF SLIME

Your nose makes a sticky, gooey fluid all the time. It's called mucus—better known as snot. Snot may look gross, but it has an important job to do. It protects the lungs. Every time you breathe through your nose, you take in dust, dirt, germs, and pollen. These things could harm your lungs.

Instead, anything that flies into your nose gets stuck in a pool of gooey mucus. Incoming particles are also caught by tiny hairs in the lining of the airway. These hairs move back and forth, making wavelike motions in the mucus. They act like a conveyor belt, sweeping any trapped particles toward the front of the nose or the back of the throat.

When the mucus mixes with dirt and other stuff from the air, it forms a "booger." A booger is basically dried-up snot. It can be big or small, slimy or crumbly. Everybody has boogers. But getting caught picking one from your nose can be really embarrassing!

When you catch a cold, your snot may get so runny that it dribbles out of your nose. That happens because your body is battling germs. Blood vessels in the nose lining get leaky. Fluid leaks out and mixes with mucus. At the same time, you might have a stuffed nose because the nose lining becomes swollen. Then there is less room for air to flow in and out. So it gets harder to breathe.

Yikes! A single sneeze may contain about 40,000 microscopic droplets. Both coughing and sneezing can spread a lot of germs.

Meanwhile, some of the mucus turns into thick, yellow globs that clog up your throat. You automatically cough or sneeze to clear that stuff out of your nose and throat.

OOZY THINGS

Do you think pus is gross? Pus is a sign of an infection. When you get a cut or scrape, bacteria can sneak inside your body. An infection happens when these bacteria start to multiply and damage your body's cells. At the first sign of trouble, the infected cells send out chemicals to alert the body's number one defenders: the white blood cells. These blood cells come to fight the invaders. When they arrive, a serious battle takes place.

White blood cells swarm over the bacteria and eat them. But the bacteria produce poisons, so white blood cells die after eating a lot of the bacteria. Pus is actually a mixture of dead white blood cells, dead bacteria, and bits of dead skin from the wound. The body keeps sending out more white blood cells until they finish killing off the bacteria. In the meantime, your skin may stay red and swollen with pus.

Would You Believe...?

If you pop a pimple, that yucky white stuff inside that oozes out is actually pus—dead white blood cells and germs.

CHAPTER SEVEN

What's That Gunk?

EARWAX

Believe it or not, earwax is not just useless gunk. For one thing, it helps to keep the ear canals smooth and moist. The ear canals are curved tubes that lead to the eardrums. Without earwax, these tubes would get dry and itchy. Earwax also traps insects, dust, and dirt so they don't go farther into the ear. Another good thing about earwax is that it contains special chemicals that help protect against germs.

Your ears never run out of earwax. Every day, special glands inside the ear canal produce the sticky, yellowish wax. This new earwax pushes the old stuff toward the outer ear. Usually, earwax dries up and falls out in tiny clumps or flakes.

Eew! (Don't Try This at Home)

In the Middle Ages, monks had a strange use for earwax. Since printing presses hadn't been invented yet, they made books by hand. Some of these books were decorated with brightly colored pictures. The monks used earwax and even urine in making their colored inks. The earwax helped the inks flow smoothly and stick to the pages.

Some doctors say, "Never put anything smaller than your elbow into your ear." Before you go nuts trying to figure out how you *can* put your elbow into your ear, we'll let you in on the secret: It's just a joke. What they mean is that you shouldn't put anything—not Q-tips, paper clips, or even your finger—into your ears to clean out earwax. You could scratch the ear canal and get it infected. You could also poke a hole in your eardrum and cause hearing loss. If too much wax builds up in your ears, you should have a doctor clean them out.

EYE BOOGERS

Doesn't "eye goo" remind you of snot? But what's it doing in your eyes? Unlike snot, that gunk in your eyes doesn't really have a purpose.

When you are awake, you blink about ten to fifteen times a minute. Your eyelids act like windshield wipers and keep your eyes clean and moist. But when you are asleep, your eyelids stay closed. A mixture of tears, sweat, and oils

builds up in the corners of your eyes. Meanwhile, bacteria grow in those nice warm, closed-in spaces under your eyelids. Your body sends bacteria-eating cells to fight them, and they add to the goo. By the time you wake up, some of this gooey gunk has dried up and become crusty.

❀ ❀ ❀ ❀

Runny noses, sticky earwax, burping, and farts—did you realize there were so many yucky things about your own body?

Your body will keep on doing yucky, slimy, gooey things for the rest of your life. Teenagers have to deal with even more yucky stuff! A surge of hormones gives them a face full of pus-filled zits, a snowfall of dandruff, and really stinky sweat.

The yucky topics we explored in this book are normal, everyday things that happen to everyone's bodies. As you get older, you might even find some new yucky things along the way!

WORDS TO KNOW

acne Frequent pimples on the skin of the face, neck, and upper back.

ammonia A chemical that is a waste product of many body processes.

bacteria Germs; single-celled organisms too small to see without a microscope. Some bacteria cause disease.

blackhead A clogged oil pore open to the air.

bladder A baglike organ in which urine (pee) is stored.

carbon dioxide A gas that is produced by the body and released in exhaled air. This gas is also used in the carbonation of soft drinks.

ear canal A curved tube leading into the ear.

eardrum A thin, vibrating covering that stretches across the opening into the middle ear.

earwax A yellowish, sticky substance produced by special glands in the ear canal.

feces Solid waste made of undigested food and intestinal bacteria; also called poop or stool.

gland An organ or group of cells that produce a substance. The substance either does a certain job in the body or passes out of the body.

hormones Chemicals that help control body activities.

infection Invasion of the body, usually by bacteria or viruses that multiply and damage tissues.

intestines Coiled, tube-like parts of the digestive tract in which food is digested and nutrients are absorbed.

motion sickness Dizziness, nausea, and other symptoms resulting when messages from the ears about position and movement contradict those from the eyes.

mucus A gooey liquid produced by cells in the lining of the nose and breathing passages.

pimple A raised sore on the skin formed by the infection of a pore.

pore An opening, especially the opening from a sweat gland, sebaceous gland, or hair follicle.

pus A whitish substance containing dead white blood cells, bacteria, and dead skin from the wound.

saliva A liquid that keeps the mouth moist and starts digesting starches; spit.

sweat glands Coiled tubes in the skin that help to cool the body and get rid of excess water and wastes.

urea An important waste product in the urine.

urine A liquid waste produced by the kidneys; pee.

vomit To force food from the stomach back out through the esophagus (food pipe) and mouth.

white blood cells Jellylike blood cells that can move through tissues and are an important part of the body's defenses. Some white blood cells eat germs and clean up bits of damaged cells and dirt.

FURTHER READING

Books

Claybourne, Anna. *The Usborne Complete Book of the Human Body*. London: Usborne Publishing Ltd, 2006.

Rosenberg, Pam. *Eew! Icky, Sticky, Gross Stuff in Your Body*. Mankato, Minn.: Child's World, 2008.

Szpirglas, Jeff. *Gross Universe: Your Guide to All Disgusting Things Under the Sun*. Toronto, Ontario: Maple Tree Press, Inc., 2004.

Internet Addresses

BrainPOP: Health. "Your Body and How It Works."
<http://www.brainpop.com/health/>

Discovery Kids: The Yuckiest Site on the Internet. "Your Gross & Cool Body."
<http://yucky.discovery.com/flash/body/>

Kids Health. "How the Body Works."
<http://kidshealth.org/kid/htbw/htbw_main_page.html>

Index

A
acne (zits), 18–19, 40
ammonia, 32

B
bacteria
    bad breath, 16–17
    farts and, 10–11
    in feces, 35
    in sweat, 12–14
    in urine, 33
bad breath, 16–17
bladder, 33
body odors, 6, 15–16
body position,
    sensing, 25–28
boogers, 37
burping, 7–9

C
carbon dioxide, 7–9
constipation, 34

D
dandruff, 23–25
diarrhea, 34

E
earwax, 41–42
eye boogers, 43–44

F
farting, 9–11
feet, smelly, 12–14
foods, 10–11, 17
fungi, 23–24

G
gas pressure, 7–11

H
hormones, 16, 18, 23

I
infection, 38–40
intestines, 10–11,
    33–35

K
kidneys, 31

M
moles, 20, 22–23
morning breath,
    16–17
motion sickness,
    25–28
mucus (snot), 36–38

P
peeing, 31–33

poop (feces), 33–35
pores, 12
pus, 19, 38–40

S
saliva, 16, 17
skin cells, 23, 24
stomach
    in burping, 8–9
    in throwing up,
        28–30
stomach acid, 29–30
sweat glands, 12–16

T
throwing up
    (vomiting), 28–30

U
urea, 32

V
viruses, 20

W
warts, 20, 21
whiteheads, 19